Sketching in the Last Light

BY
HANNY LINN

ISBN: 979-8-218-84795-1
This paperback edition first published in 2025

For Victor.
I'm the kite, you're the line.
thank you

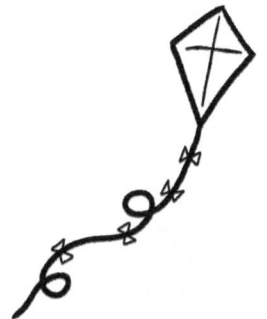

Table of Contents

HEAT WAVES AND SUGAR HIGHS

COOL BREEZE AND LEAF BONES

GREY SKIES AND COLD LIGHT

BLUSH DAWN AND BUD SONGS

HEAT WAVES
AND
SUGAR HIGHS

Imprint

When I was young,
I loved to draw in crayon,
unaware the marks
would hardly stay on

through machines
with vicious cleaning spins.
All my artwork
ended up in bins.

Later on in life,
the feeling lingers
that the colors
melting on my fingers

never had a chance
to last at all.
All my work is fated
to be small.

Yet I cannot stop
the eager rate
at which my hands
seem destined to create,

tracing in impressions
stained and lame
inky fingerprints
that spell my name.

Natalie Horn

Sugar Spun

Daylight rests like sugar on my tongue.
Sweet, it lingers, small and honey-dipped.
Laughter sticks like syrup in my tum,
cotton candy warming in my grip.

Kissing while we wait for bread to bake,
pop rock pecks light up like firework flares.
Both our kittens greet us when we wake,
velvet fur absorbing all our cares.

Insignificant, these moments flee
out a window opened to the breeze.
All I do is watch them, helplessly,
shrinking further in growing degrees.

Stoic, they ignore my graver pleas,
winding out until the feeling's gone.
Frantically I rush to savor these
sugar moments melting on my tongue.

Subterranean

You're underneath my skin so deep
I think of you like needle-ink
or blood that's pooled beneath the brink
of veins. You're subterranean.

You're part of me - my favorite piece.
So deeply lodged beneath my skin
I've lost where I begin and end,
like we share one flesh between us.

We are blood vessels wound so tight
to split would become suicide,
a cleavered flesh-chunk from my side,
the heart itself, both yours and mine
my organ pump, abandoned, dried,
and left outside my body.

Sunburn

My skin has turned a crusted red,
soaked in the sun of what we said together.
It tingles when I put a finger on it.
White marks bloom then shrink from scarlet.

In the moment we did not feel the need
to stop and lather up ourselves in sunscreen.
After all,
any second, we were leaving.

Then you stayed
and
so did I.

Like a line of ants, the sun crawled through the sky.

It stuck us to our chairs
like candy melted to our seats
with cider sips and storied dreams.

We could not give it up,
the moment spent in burning sun,
refusing precious minutes for sunblock.
Now I glimpse my tendered flesh
and do not regret it yet,
treasuring instead our heartfelt talk.

Erasure

I create a vision in my head
of who I wish I was.
Curls committed to my whole head,
eye-bags melted by frankincense and pepper oil,
legs toned with runner's discipline
and abs to boot.

I would erase my laughter lines,
meals shared in love,
the desk job rooting my legs to the floor.
I would sterilize myself until I'm plastic,
perfect in my inexperience.

We Are Women

To sit among a group of girls
is to talk about your mother
like a shared memory
and hear back in sing-song tones,
"mine too!"

We see beyond shapes,
our sympathies to the sculptures we made
when we were told
what frames our bodies should resemble
to mean something.

We are puzzle pieces
charmed by every homely contour
but our own.

One day,
the urge to shrink will die
and in its place
will grow a space
full of white-hot voices
inflating our lungs,
balloons in the sky that cannot help
but rise.

Lexi Sánchez

Sunset Cowboy

We gather round and spill tears.
They slide down sweet
but turn bitter
when they hit home in our hearts
like honey whiskey
or soda sat too long outside.

We send off a cowboy
to catch the sunset.
We hear our voices ask
in spite of ourselves,
"Can't you stay for one more game?"

But it is time, it is time.

He rides away.
We watch his shadow spreading over the ground
in a way we will remember.
We can still see all the things it touched
even after he crests the last hill.
It was giant, after all.

The sun is setting into quiet grey.
Dark and cold for now,
we will wait for the sun
to rise once more
on the day we meet again.

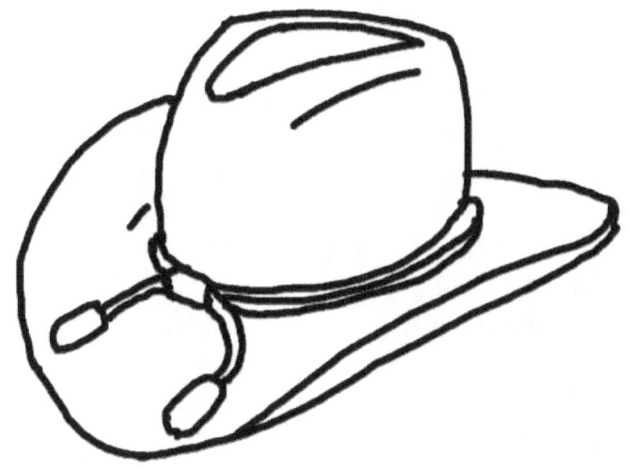

Victor Lineros

Keeper

Once she was a pretty thing.
Now it cannot help but sting
seeing how my life has come to shape her.

Never where I hope she'll be,
Chunky, fat, and frustrating,
I continue in my quest to shrink her.

She is worn, and wrinkled, too,
full of veins in sickened blue
like an accent color that won't suit her.

She's a pudgy, rounded shape,
full of flaws I've grown to hate
in the constant war I fight against her.

If she split clean off my bones
and my soul at last was lone,
I would happily never pursue her.

At least, years back, I had this view.
Over time my vision's skewed
all because of him. He doesn't hate her.

He is blind or sees unclear,
or he doesn't seem to fear
all the little uglinesses in her.

Miracle! He doesn't mind
lumpy, wrinkled, ill-designed
forms; in fact he rather seems to like her.

Wrinkles formed from years of bliss
blush beneath my lover's kiss
when he looks beyond the years that changed her.

In decoding what he sees,
she's re-born a mystery,
hiding secret treasures deep within her

as if superficial traits
bear far less than all the weight
I in my disgust attribute to her.

Somehow seeing through his eyes
that she has become a prize
casts an air of loveliness about her.

Not my first pick in the line,
but beloved through his eyes,
I have come to feel a fondness for her.

Dressed by love and beauty crowned,
aging by the man I've found,
after all this time, I think I'll keep her.

Thread

Flexible I find this thread,
limp one moment, strong the next,
tightly wrapped around my ribs and yours.

Always growing is the thread,
thickening as time weaves webs,
spinning years that layer more and more.

Comforting, this welcome thread,
closing distance in its stead
until there's no space between our cores.

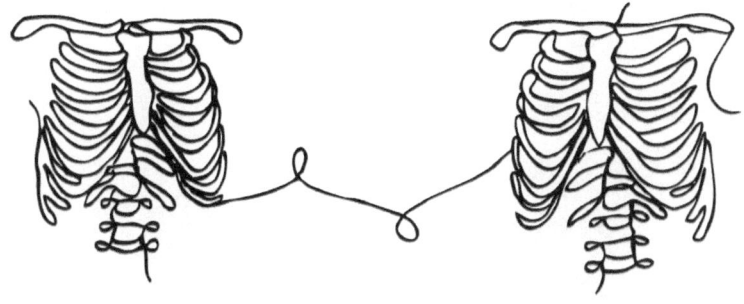

Elisa Fisher

Forest Fire

How can you stand by and idly watch
homes and humans eaten up by flames,
scarred by fires of greed you put in place,
thinking they will stop or else be tamed?

Power-hungry lions sink their teeth
into tender necks of helpless beasts.
By what logic did you tell yourself
you would be kept safely from their feasts?

Bedtime Stories

Weave me tales of magic, bright,
with a glow that dims the night,
something beautiful and light,
mystical enchantments.

Feed me tales of castles, old,
full of knights, the wise and bold,
noble cheer to banish cold,
safe inside their fortress.

Paint me tales of people, strong,
pushing back on all that's wrong,
single-minded in the throng,
strong and righteous warriors.

Sing me tales of ladies, fair,
bidding those around to care,
eager for the world's repair,
draped in queenly mercy.

Gift me tales of noble kings,
keeping safe beneath their wings
even lowly, humble things,
stately in their justice.

Tell me tales of times long gone,
formed by hope and peace and brawn,
dreams to lay my head upon.
Fill my head with stories.

Parachute Big Top

My life is the downbeat
in the kindergarten circus game.
Plastic sinks around me
and my future is obscured by hands
grasping at my prospects and attentions,
hiding what is true.

Life pulls in a rhythm,
every measured beat resolves the same.
Then an unseen signal
stirs a frenzy into white-red bands,
warring futures pulling out-of-sync to
win this children's game.

Fate, in quickened chaos,
loves to yank and thrash the parachute
low then high then sideways,
my potential helpless to withstand
all the fevered plot twists pinched and hidden
in its tight-gripped hand.

Finally, I loosen
up my hold on all my plans for me.
In the momentary
freedom is a quick, retreating view
of a figure standing in the tent point,
holding safe what's true.
Steadfast through the chaos of my life:
I suspect it's you.

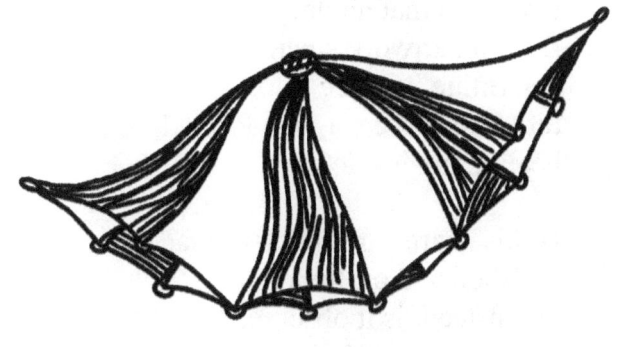

Michaela Baker

Mosaic

Do the wind-swept words I make
patterned in the sand
have some lasting force at all,
scattered on the land?
If they fade out over time
as the years expand,
are they still worth letting slip
from my clenching hand?

If my castles made of sand
scatter with the tide,
are they somehow less worthwhile
than ones that abide?
Does an artwork's permanence
determine its price,
rather than the way it's formed-
healing me inside?

Is this heartshard that I've made
polished and on-trend?
Or, instead, is it obscure,
what my words intend?
Are my inner thoughts and fears
something like a friend
to the people that will read
all that I have penned?

Fragments of this thing I've made,
sharpened bits of glass,
gleam in cruel condemning ways -
pieces of my past.

Ugly flecks in certain light
where they lay in mass
bounce a fractured picture back,
tarnishing like brass.

With fresh insight looking down
on the glittered pile,
I acknowledge angles that
shade it less than vile.
Is creation of itself,
like fragments of tile,
beautiful in brokenness,
always worth the while?

If this rough sketch of my life
finds some way to reach
kindred humans on their quest
to what they believe,
I'll resist the urge to let
months of quiet speech
rot unwitnessed in my mind,
sand specks on a beach.

Gathering a breath before
diving in the deep,
I bend down to offer up
for the world's critique
my imperfect sketchbook songs
gathered at my feet.
Every sliver I give up
is some piece of me.

COOL BREEZE
AND
LEAF BONES

Candle-Making

The shadows in their tendency to bleed
have overcome my space. I feel the need
to make a mark against their brutal skin.
I wrestle with my hands, then they begin
to push against the bleakness and the gloom
that overflow the corners of my room.

I light a candle and the twilight blurs.
Like waking up from sleep, my feelings stir
to see a thing so fragile casting light
against the rolling onslaught of the night.
I will mirror its recalcitrant aim
to make, if for a moment,
fragile flame.

Sarah Mullins

Real Girls

My heart quivers in my ribs
at the thought of all the mothers
telling their daughters
what to eat,
how much to put
into themselves,
or take out,
until they are "just right" -
flesh-and-bone dolls
in a world they made up.

Maybe if they knew we carve ourselves
out of wood,
thinning ring by ring
until we are puppets,
paper-thin,
they would hesitate
on the next axe swing.

Then again,
maybe they think
to be frail
is beautiful.

The Trade

I would rather age my cheeks
from too-often grinning,
than sit picture-pure for years,
never quite beginning.

I would rather jump, afraid,
fearing a bellyflop
than sit silent down below
dreaming about the top.

I would rather wail in pain,
overcome by my grief,
than be still and solemn when
those gone too quickly leave.

I would rather feel the ache
from uphill inclining
than be met with apathy
at my own enshrining.

I would rather make a mess,
constantly forgiving,
than sit faultless through my life,
too perfect for living.

Worn

The sleeve of my jacket is starting to fray.
It was used when I bought it
But now that I've got it,
I'm wearing its fabric away.

I use it to hide all my changes in weight.
It fits when I'm thin
or I'm eating again.
It never cares how much I ate.

I like that its pockets are fur-lined and deep.
It holds all my trinkets,
my shame and my secrets,
and covers my eyes when I weep.

Its fabric is thick and its buttons are brass.
I thought it eternal,
All others infernal
and simply just not made to last.

It wasn't avoidable, this chilling day.
I know people leave.
Still, it hurts
when the sleeve
of my jacket is starting to fray.

Zombie

I did not know suffering
until I was reanimated.
All my death, I lived inside
a cemetery, stone-wall gated,
taking on the shape
of my own grave.

My skeleton was brittle and I didn't know

it was held together by
the coffin that kept it.
I sighed, looked around,
and no longer accepted
this prison of stone
where my body was brought.
I rose to get up
on my legs full of rot.

My skeleton was brittle and I didn't know.

My corpse began to fall apart,
too brittle was my weakened heart,
unused to what it takes to live,
leaking feelings like a sieve,
overcome by all the aching.
Now I stand - unearthed and breaking.

My skeleton was brittle and I didn't know.

The Cliff

There is a mind cliff where I sometimes look,
unable to resist its gravity,
on a ledge-rock, calm, until I'm shook
perilously unsure, balancing.

For long stretches, I will let myself think
I've escaped the hypnosis of its call.
Then I find myself stood at the brink;
how I got there, I cannot recall.

Like a spell whose bid calls up from the void,
some force locks my legs. I can't turn away.
Time stops as I crawl forward, annoyed,
topside staring down its empty grey.

Once I tried to fashion a kind of wall,
tall enough to hide the pit from my view
but the tireless droning of its call
pushed the wall down with a strength renewed.

I fear it will hunt me throughout my days,
never fully gone, but sometimes unseen,
lurking in the blind-spot of my gaze,
waiting to reveal a fresh ravine.

I imagine slipping off of the edge,
easy into darkness where I am still,
every question answered in the dredge
raking murky waters of my will.

Fascinated by its unending depths,
I feel fear like vultures ready to dive.
It will carve me hollow, steal my breaths,
unless it admits I'm still alive.

Easy isn't brave and fixed is not peace.
Reluctant, I make myself take the road
uphill and away, and I release
feeling there's some surety I am owed.

Lifelong will this battle rage of our might,
victories, though hard won, are of no note,
since I know soon there will come a night
I'm lost in the labyrinth of its throat.

Daylight with a mighty power can shrink
parts of the foul cliff away from my sight.
Though I always hear its call to sink,
equally I heed the nudge to fight.

My days and years will inch like bird-food by,
until at the end of all my striving
time in its reluctance then to fly
will declare this dance
my surviving.

Tree Bark

As kids we flex our rubber-banded souls,
not yet encumbered by the weight of truth
or one-way hopes, or disillusioned goals:
the precious elasticity of youth.

Our pale green stems are pliant and take shape
wherever we are planted, then we grow,
healing when we gain wood bark scars and scrapes
not yet conscious of the marks that we show.

As adults, we have hardened up like trees
whose sunken roots are melding to the earth.
Our trunks cannot be shifted by the breeze,
the woodgrain marred and ringed within our girth.

Long years spent in the choices we have made
have worn down our propensity to change.

Afraid of the Dark

There's a dark spot in my brain
where my psyche has free reign
to create a hellish scene.
I can't help the things I see.

Chairs and tables, hanging drapes
morph into foreboding shapes -
skeletons with pitch black eyes,
demons bent on my demise,
skinny men with missing lips,
crones with bloodied fingertips,
wraith-like, hooded, hungry ghosts
creeping toward my bed frame posts.

As I mumble prayers for sleep
from my vile designs that sweep
across the floor, above my head,
right beside me on the bed,
staring back from empty eyes,
hushing all my voiceless cries,
I will give a silent scream
hoping that it's just a dream.

Stab

I can toss like dagger-knives
words to shred and ruin lives,
seeking heat and tender skin,
something soft to burrow in.

Once my words have left my lips,
I can't help the prick that nips
and bites like jagged metal tips,
spiraled from my loosened grip.

Some words shank off harmlessly.
Some will find their mark and sink
deep within the tender grey
making up my rival's brain.

Once they're thrown, they won't return,
doomed instead to scorch and burn
anyone within their path
as they roil and churn with wrath.

Missiles, they will seek the heat
left by insecurities,
pain points bruised and not-yet healed,
on display and too revealed.

Wounding words will double down
in the open scars they've found,
bringing to the surface there
fears that lay in disrepair.

I'm a killer, or a shark,
satisfied to hit my mark,
quickened by the sight of blood,
loosing havoc like a flood.

Little did I know the slits
made by my offhanded hits
in my prey were mirrored in
my own unprotected skin.

Like a wolf that licks a blade,
hungry for the blood it made,
with a sharpened sword of glee,
I have lacerated
me.

Learning to Read Music

Desperately I crave the language
to describe the tune I hear.
Hungrily, I chase the notes
that form the tune,
though they're unclear.

Hopefully, despite frustration,
I force fingertips to keys
aching for imagined chords
that form my muse,
a sweet release.

Calculated patterns, metered-out
and stacked, adorn the page.
They will circulate my mind
annoyingly.

I quit in rage.

sketch by author

43

Tricks and Treats

This time of year is mystic
when nighttime sparks with candle light
and grinning pumpkins and mysteries.

Groups of giddy adventurers
don their costumes
and face the horrors on their street
together in anonymity,
bravened when they band together.

Mist bubbles from cauldrons.
They brew something special,
like a secret,
and maybe there's magic inside their cast-iron walls
strong enough to beat back
death and darkness and demons.

For a night we believe it can be done.

Orange lights twinkle in spiderwebs and skulls,
laughing at death.
Disguises embolden all to face from the safety
of a fabric mask
the true horrors of this life.

How palatable it all becomes,
as if death is nothing more than
plastic bones
arranged on neighbors' porches,
as if you can put it aside the next day,
pack it up in boxes marked for the season

stuck in the cabinet
somewhere out-of-view all other days of the year.

We pretend that monsters rise from their graves
on one night only
and then return to the earth they were spat from,
safely buried until next year.
We make-believe that
we do not still see their shadows
behind us in the street.

We believe we can hide beneath the face of
a villain,
a hero,
a monster,
a prince,
and that no one will know
underneath
we are afraid.

What a marvelous trick.

Quiet Days

I used to fear quiet days,
loud thoughts filling
silences in my mind's conversations.

Now the slow days
are like frosting -
pops of cake sugar,
sweet breath between plunges.

My quiet days are full of hopeful choices,
waiting patiently,
half-drunk mugs on a windowsill,
hungry for my free time.

It is a luxury to drink them slowly.

Antonio Gonzalez

Murky Plant Water

I changed the water for my plant
and now its leaves have drooped,
as if they had some private strength
when roots in secret grouped.

Dirty water cleaned and tossed,
its lengthy leaves scrubbed pure,
my plant at last was new and fresh,
exposed in its allure.

I wondered if its grime and grit
had somehow made it bold
and now, uncovered to the world,
its tender shoots are cold.

Perhaps the ugliness in life,
akin to plantish goop,
serves to make our root balls strong
so that our leaves don't droop.

GREY SKIES
AND
COLD LIGHT

Trapping Winter (a sevenling)

We are eager to lay out our things-
snowflakes, string-light trees and candy canes,
hoping our impatience doesn't scare

winter from its cautious drawing-near.
Drawn like bees to honeyed homes and cheer
hearth-heat lures the season to our snare.

We will hunt it like a grizzly bear.

First Night of Winter

A little dust of snow
shivers over fallen leaves
left in yellowed pockets of earth.

The shift in seasons -
wind-blown breath,
coaxes us to move lest we freeze over,
bones stirring up reluctant but eager
to move in protest to death.

sketch by author

Void Boat

There are some parts of me that crave unchanging ground,
unyielding notions that I've found
are true each time I have the patience to see them.

Rival parts of me consider the truth afloat,
and step into an unmanned boat
curiously looking into clouded water.

I am afraid to lose my grip on what is real
and in the aftermath, to feel
myself unmoored and drifting farther from the docks.

Torn between curiosity and my restraint,
waves below me tempt self-constraint
and I consider relativity and faith.

Perception ripples, ever-changing what I think,
and I am pulled toward the brink,
helpless to resist imagining a quick plunge.

If I boldly meet the watery depths below,
and find my face reflected, lone,
the underlying emptiness would destroy me.

A Sudden Snow

Oftentimes I find snow had a hand in
redefining dead lands within its glow.
Withered trees I thought lay long abandoned
gain fresh beauty shielding a fragile snow.

Lonely, brittle wood afraid to splinter,
if it can withstand the chill and the frost,
will find there is beauty yet in winter
gilding haunted stumps of what has been lost.

Some small life force shivers and wakes pining,
filling hollowed trunks with new glittered hope.
Leafless branches now are girded shining,
trimmed in snowflake fur like kingly white robes.

Turning from despair there is a calling
rousing trees to life when snow's found falling.

Snowglobe

I can't help my snow globe brain.
Thoughts will still then stir again.

Words melt on my fingerprints
faster than Olympic sprints.

I can't stop them going quick -
snow that lands but doesn't stick.

sketch by author

Anxiety

From the hall, my bedroom sings a siren-song this night.
Burning off their energy, my cats begin to fight
before at last, they make their peace
and wind themselves up tight.

Husband chats with me about the life-sized bites of day
spinning in his mind that he's got looping on replay.
As we talk the daylight morphs
from blue to deepened gray.

Cat-tails curl protectively around two sleeping faces.
At my feet they lay asleep in their respective places.
Curtains drawn and nightlight on,
I recite my graces.

Husband stills a lengthened breath as he gives in to sleep.
Only I, awake at night, my thoughts like secrets keep,
cursed to flounder on my own
above the dreamless deep.

Insomniac

I have got a date with sleep.
I am hoping that he'll keep
his promise to not run late
since he loves to make me wait.

We will flirt throughout the day
but he never seems to stay
when it really matters most.
Still, he haunts me like a ghost.

I slide into bed unsure
if the shape beyond my door
will at last enter the room
or will ever only loom

out-of-reach throughout the night.
He makes me wait out of spite.
Finally, I see his face,
never tiring of this chase.

Restless, heavy, fading fast,
all I hope is that he'll last
through the starlight's fleeting glow
and resist the urge to go.

Ever-hunting, like a shark,
he leaves while it is still dark,
seeking out some fairer prey.
I am left alone, awake.

Insecurity

It flickered - flame made up of night.
Its hollow shadows carve a blight
that once I thought had left my mind,
but here,
I find it restless lies.

Hidden like a blade in its sheath,
doubt was waiting deep underneath.
My layers of confidence, discreet,
are pierced
by its unyielding teeth.

It will ruin all I have made,
perverting every accolade,
darkening my pride in its shade,
my mind
bewildered and betrayed.

Things I had loved crack in flashes,
notes, songs, sketches - burnt to ashes,
caught in doubt's relentless thrashes,
asking,
"Don't you know what trash is?"

Quietly I feel myself hush.
I hope I can evade its crush.
Merciless, it hunts out my flush
like blood,
and paints on shame like blush.

Frozen without sails on a ship,
seeking solid ground, I will slip,
unable to dull its sharpened tip
my neck
is slit beneath its grip.

Torchbearer

There was a torch in the trench today.
Sky tones blushed with dawn's ombre,
dimming black to palest grey,
flickering a moment.

Tiny flames blinked in the night,
torchlight growing in its fight
to encase the hills in light,
echoing the rally.

Embers flickered in my chest.
As I watched the light fade west
I resolved to try my best
to maintain this cinder.

Stalled

Tentative, I tiptoe steps
along the cliffside ridge line,
mimicking the shape
my life
has formed -
a slickened incline.

Through the years, I've felt the need
to claim the name "impressive"
but in trying to
achieve
such fame
I've grown obsessive.

Feeling pressure to not fail,
eager, despite risk, to please,
I'm afraid to slip
or fall
backwards
or, helpless, to freeze.

Weakening, my calves protest
as I stand undecided,
wondering if all
my steps
thus far
have been misguided.

Uncertain and unwilling
to progress, I linger here
searching for the strength
it takes
to fight
to push past my fear.

Winter Trap

It stalks us slowly.
The air is
chilled.

The sky is sunless.
We shiver,
thrilled.

Fall starts to panic,
plans,
unfulfilled.

It's gaining on us,
lethally
skilled.

Winter approaches.
Snowflakes are
spilled.

It muffles footsteps.
Our storms are
stilled.

Forced into stillness,
the year's
fulfilled.

Snow Catena Rondo

Frozen white is winter's plea to rest.
Snow like siren's singing drifts along,
casting spells of stillness in its song.
Frozen white is winter's plea to rest.

Snow like siren's singing drifts along.
Earth herself is dusted in a dream,
velvet layered white as thickened cream.
Snow like siren's singing drifts along.

Earth herself is dusted in a dream.
Frozen white is winter's plea to rest,
held like lullabies in mother's chest.
Earth herself is dusted in a dream.

Frozen white is winter's plea to rest.
Snow like siren's singing drifts along,
casting spells of stillness in its song.
Frozen white is winter's plea to rest.

Winding Down

Nighttime embarks, quiet and still,
spinning mental wheels until
thoughts in wearied measures slow,
worries burn and flicker low,
stuck in my molasses mind,
stiffened by a drowsy bind,
protesting a final peep
then, defeated, lost to sleep.

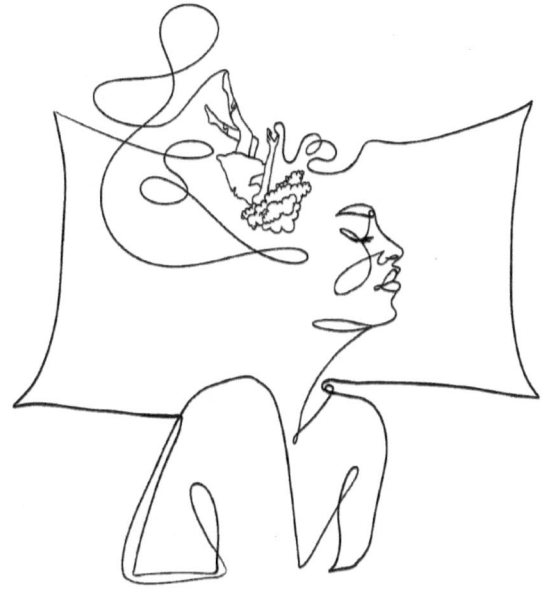

Gracey Vaughn

BLUSH DAWN
AND
BUD SONGS

A Warming Day

I cannot stop the years from slipping by
like bits of snow that melt beneath my hand,
eager to dissolve the more I try
to keep them sheltered from the heat's demand.

Years like tear trails bleed into the ground;
strength and beauty flee in vicious theft.
Though unlikely, when it melts, I've found
snow rejoices with the time that's left.

Bouncing light with fervor to the trees,
snow paints earth in growing shades of dawn.
It will dance like diamonds on the breeze,
catch a glimpse of sun, and then it's gone.

Maybe if I still and face the sun,
I will melt in peace, when I am done.

Thaw

There are moments when the glow
from the friends I love and know,
like the cheer of mistletoe,
seems to thaw and melt me.

Instinct dictates I withdraw
so that no one sees me thaw,
as if feeling were a flaw
I should be ashamed of.

Though I try in vain to freeze,
kinship is a warming breeze
loosening my heart with ease,
strengthening me for it.

There's a beauty, being known
by the ones who, too, have grown
on the path where I've been thrown.
I am grateful for it.

Thinking through what I've been dealt,
it's a privilege to melt.
I am humbled to have felt
warming, lifelong friendships.

Ode to Spring Crowns

Once you stood skeletal, colorless, grey,
frozen awaiting the blush of the day.
Warming cold branches that shrink from the glow,
springtime is giving you courage to grow.

Quietly hardy, you're strong at the core.
Winter has taught you to not hope for more
than outlasting hunger, sickness, and droughts,
safely protecting your tenderest sprouts.

Now I can see you are thawing again.
Inside your refuge you're housing a wren.
Strength in your branches has grown them out long.
Bold with fresh trust, birds are bursting in song.

No longer fearing the hunter's sharp knife
prey can find peace in your lighthouse of life.
There in your fingers I think I see green -
Though it is shy, I am glad that it's seen.

It's been so long since we've witnessed your joy.
Thaw yourself quickly so we can enjoy
your hard-won fruits and the comfort you bring,
glowing from hope that survived everything,

Seeing you crowned is like new buds in spring.

Decision Fatigue

I have much to do in this cyclical night
but not enough time for my mind to decide
on which story to write or which project to start,
to learn a new skill or to try a new art.

There's cleaning or writing or scrolling online,
finally learning some graphic design.
Maybe my time would be valued in chores,
purging my bookcases, closets, and drawers.

I could plan the week's menu, or start on my laundry,
or maybe start training to hike up Mt.Quandary.
My free time is precious, these hours too few
to make up my mind on what task I should do.

I run through my choices like hoops in my head,
then stuck and exhausted I crawl into bed.

The Bamboo Plant in my Room

I stare at the plant in my room every night.
I'm amazed at its height
and the way it will fight
in its daily resistance to ending up dead.
All its leaves have turned red
and its roots are unfed.

I admit the effect that the plant has is strange,
for its leaves will not fade,
it refuses to change,
pushing upwards and outwards with nothing to lose,
like it can't help but choose
to ignore my abuse
and to bloom in defiance of pain.

sketch by author

Maypole

I heard remnants of your words
in my brain, amassing.
Far from strangers in my mind,
they were not trespassing;
Rather, they found space in my
scatterbrained grey matter
as if by some miracle
they preferred the latter.

My mind is a second-home
to your thoughts and wordplay.
Sharing years of life has formed
this familiar highway.
Just when I believe our minds
cannot be brought nearer,
you reflect my thoughts to me
like a mental mirror.

Like a springtime dawning day
when the sky grows lighter,
we are ropes around a pole,
growing ever tighter.

Journals

We're born unlined,
our covers new
and undefined.
We wait for life
and, patient, find
our journals fill
with flashbacks, vined
ink soaking through
the thoughts we bind.

Patterns will wind
through the pages
that form our minds,
some in chalk or
pen-dipped designs
so they won't be
poorly-defined
when the years will
start to unwind.

Void of their lines
journals fill when
they have some time,
full of what we
love and enshrine
or the pain that
stiffens our spines
until we are
at last, defined.

Brave Flowers

Fields of flowers,
lithe and frail,
push past soil and gloom,
opening their pastel petals
in their bravened bloom.

Do the tender
springtime buds,
naked and uncrowned,
hesitate to leave their safety
nestled in the ground?

Slow momentum
is their spell,
spreading and rooting;
wildflowers will dress the earth with
the briefest beauty.

They want only
for the warmth
of sun in the sky,
letting goodness feed them even
though they're doomed to die.

Strong but fragile,
like the buds -
I can hope and strive
for the sort of courage flowers
have to be alive.

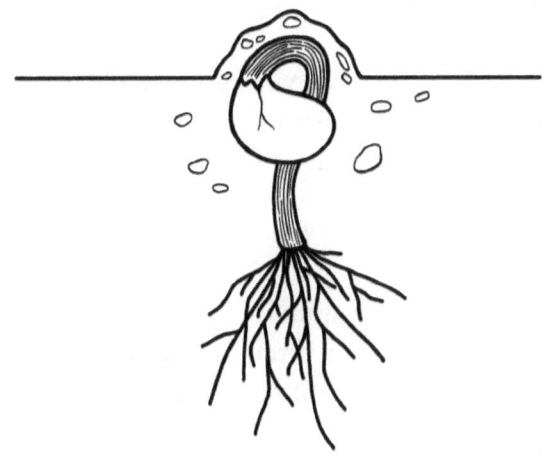

Rae Jefferson

Existential Houseplant

What is the point of the plant in my room?
Is it attempting to brighten the gloom?
Often-forgotten, in darkness, unfed -
according to google
my plant should be dead.

Doesn't it know age is lining its branches
with ugly white scars just as long as its branch is?
Isn't it shamed by the sag in its florets?
My plant should be pitied,
the way I ignore it.

Doesn't it feel that its prospects are wretched,
or is it ashamed that it hasn't affected
the room that could take it or leave it to die?
Where does it summon
the courage to try?

Growing impossibly despite its chances,
steady in spite of its grim circumstances,
my plant wastes no time on self-centered glances.
I am amazed as it,
faithful, advances.

Maybe its goal is to reach for the ceiling,
past the poor paint job that's already peeling
and gaze there instead toward a view more appealing,
fixed in its hope for
eventual healing.

Its lack of clear purpose is troubling to me.
It's undeterred in its futility.
Its virtues are puzzling, that little tree.
I can't help but feel it will
start changing me.

Trunk and Branches

Once I thought that humans
drift like leaves upon the breeze.
Now I think that people grow and
shape themselves like trees.

All we see are wood and leaves,
parts of greater sums,
not the sap of life lived thick,
pulsing soft like drums.

Down below are brooding roots,
secrets undiscussed -
pain we bear and hometown hurt -
what's been done to us.

Bark and skin adorn our frame
keeping soft bits sound,
bold enough to face whatever
challenges abound.

Names get carved into our trunks -
marks for those we love
carried skyward as we age
in our crowns above.

Imminent is how we age,
expanding tip to base,
unable to resist our growth
moving up through space,
hoping in our journey
to encounter simple grace.

sketch by author

Tattoo Artist

I plead with the world
to let me tattoo it,
along its scar tissue
and under and through it.

I think it's afraid
and I know that it's nervous
to have someone poking
'round under the surface.

I see its deep wounds,
its abuse and mistrust,
all the places where fear
lays corroded with rust.

I hardly can blame it
for what it's been through.
I talk to it gently
about its tattoo.

I'll point it at someone
who sees more than skin,
who's eager to heal it
when we first begin.

Its ruin is not
quite as bad as it sounded.
In fact, we will leave it
fairer than we found it.

There's beauty in heartbreak,
like stones dressed in moss
with bright shades of healing,
this beauty from loss.

I hope I can mark it
with flowers and trees,
with beauty and kindness,
with love songs and peace.

I'm eager to transfer
new faith in good things,
restore the world's softness
like true hoping brings.

I'll hold its hand gently
and count down to three,
then show the world's people
the beauty I see,
so thankful it trusted
its heart scars to me.

A Psalm

How pleasantly the lines of life
have laid for me,
in patterns I could hardly see
before my journey shaped them.

I could not form a better, more
for-me design
than He who dictates every line
and lovingly has placed them.

ILLUSTRATION ACKNOWLEDGEMENTS

This book was a pipe dream for many months, but the moment I saw it come to life is one that I owe largely to the amazing artists that helped to illustrate it.

I count myself lucky to have met an incredible amount of talented creatives throughout my life, and even luckier to be able to call them my friends. I selfishly took the opportunity when putting this book together to commission as many of them as were able, to create artwork for me, and I could not be more thrilled with the results.

Thank you deeply to everyone who contributed illustrations to this book. This book, being my first, is one I will forever hold as a deeply personal thing, and it is made even more precious to me by the contributions of the following artists.

In order of appearance with their related poem titles, the artists featured in this book are as follows:

Imprint
Natalie Horn
@art_fanatics_shop

We Are Women
Lexi Sánchez
@lexoreno.art

Sunset Cowboy
Victor Lineros

Thread
Elisa Fisher
@ElisaFisherPhotography

Parachute Big Top
Michaela Baker

Candle-Making
Sarah Mullins
@sarah.runs.dallas

Quiet Days
Antonio Gonzalez
@tonythetiger

Winding Down
Gracey Vaughn
@leona.studios

Brave Flowers
Rae Jefferson
@raejefferson

ACKNOWLEDGEMENTS

This book started as a collection of poems written in my journal over the course of a single year. It would probably have stayed that way (as unseen scraps of paper collected in a worn notebook), without the encouragement and support of the following people.

Victor Lineros, thank you for supporting me and letting me chase my silly little dreams. You're a constant source of encouragement, stability, and inspiration. I literally could not have created this book without you.

To my friends and family, thank you for being muses in every day moments and for not shying away from me when I approach and ask them, "I've been writing poems, would you like to see?"

To Vanessa Dreme, thank you for looking over my words when they were still being formed and giving me encouraging notes to help this book solidify into what it is now.

To the members of my Clairvoyage semester, thank you for being a weekly source of accountability and motivation. I don't know if I would have made it this far into the process of self-publishing a book, or finished anything at all, without the need to report progress to the slack every week.